TALKING
WITH
ARTISTS

• •

VOLUME TWO

TALKING WITH ARTISTS

VOLUME TWO

Conversations with

Thomas B. Allen • Mary Jane Begin
Floyd Cooper • Julie Downing • Denise Fleming
Sheila Hamanaka • Kevin Henkes • William Joyce
Maira Kalman • Deborah Nourse Lattimore
Brian Pinkney • Vera B. Williams
and David Wisniewski

compiled and edited by
PAT CUMMINGS

Simon & Schuster Books for Young Readers

SIMON & SCHUSTER BOOKS FOR YOUNG READERS
An imprint of Simon & Schuster Children's Publishing Division
1230 Avenue of the Americas, New York, NY 10020

The text for this book is set in 14 point Garamond Three.
Manufactured in the U.S.A.
First edition
1 3 5 7 9 10 8 6 4 2

LIBRARY OF CONGRESS CATALOGING-IN-PUBLICATION DATA

Talking with artists.
Vol. 2-   published: New York:
Simon & Schuster Books for Young Readers.
Includes bibliographical references.
Summary: Distinguished picture book artists talk about their
early art experiences, answer questions most frequently asked by
children, and offer encouragement to aspiring artists.
ISBN: 0-689-80310-9
1. Illustrators—United States—Biography—Juvenile literature.
[1. Illustrators. 2. Artists.]
I. Cummings, Pat.
NC975.T34   1991
741.6'42'092273   [B]   91-9982
ISBN 0-02-724245-5 (v. 1)

For my mother,
Christine Taylor Cummings

CONTENTS

•• •• •• •• •• •• •• •• •• •• •• •• •• •• •• •

Dear Reader,

Many things can make your artwork better. Every artist in this book does something a little differently from the way that I would do it. They all have one thing in common, though: They keep trying new things. It might be new color combinations or patterns, or maybe they'll try new techniques. Sometimes experiments can turn out so well that you want to frame them. Sometimes they should be crumpled up and tossed to the cat. But everything you try teaches you something, even if you just find out what *doesn't* work.

In the first *Talking with Artists* fourteen artists answered eight questions about how they do the illustrations for their picture books. Those questions came straight from letters I've received and from students I've met who like making art.

For this second volume, I asked thirteen more illustrators who use a variety of materials and work in many different styles to answer these same questions. This time, among their pictures you'll also see what their work spaces look like. And what's really great is that they each reveal a secret technique you can try out for yourself. Some of the "secrets" might be ones that you've already learned . . . but I think you'll find a surprise or two as well.

The illustrators you are about to meet have all faced challenges in their work. I know I used to hate to draw hands. "Practice makes perfect!" my parents said, so I decided to draw hands until I got them right. I drew hands from magazines and cartoons; I must have drawn my own hands about a million times. I looked at hands drawn by other artists to see how they did it. I may never draw hands *perfectly,* but now I *love* to draw them and they don't seem quite so hard.

I recently got some advice from a young artist named Kali. She said that to be a good artist you must do three things: 1. *You have to concentrate,* 2. *You don't need anyone bothering you,* and 3. *Stay in the lines.* If you enjoy art, I certainly agree that you should concentrate on it and not let anyone stop you. I don't think you always need to stay in the lines, though. And, I would add this: Keep trying new things.

—Pat Cummings

Thomas B. Allen

BIRTHDAY: January 23, 1928
Thomas B. Allen

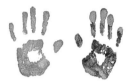

MY STORY

Growing up during the Great Depression of the 1930s meant, for most kids, having to make up their own ways of having fun. When I was six years old, my Christmas gifts under the tree were a few World War I lead soldiers, some modeling clay, and a puppy named Pal from my Granddaddy Burt. I duplicated the tiny soldiers with modeling clay, uniforms and all, and Pal chewed them up. Pal was my constant companion for twelve years.

My family lived right on the edge of Nashville. Across the gravel street were the "big hill" and the "big field" and the "big creek." Behind the field and across the creek were woods. It was in those places that we played cowboys and Indians and one-eyed cat baseball (using rocks for bases), caught salamanders and tadpoles, made tree houses and forts, and set traps for rabbits, which we never caught. On rainy days I mostly drew pictures on the scratch pads my dad brought home from his office. *The Baseball Player* [see page 12] was drawn on such a pad when I was seven. Home plate is backward but his eye is on the ball.

My mother found an art teacher for me when I was nine. There was no children's class so I drew and painted among adults every Saturday during the school year and three days a week in the summer. Living on the edge of Nashville allowed me to take the streetcar into town for art classes and ride my bicycle in the other direction to my granddaddy's farm. The classes ended when I was fourteen and I didn't study art again until I went away to art school in Chicago at the age of twenty.

But I can't remember when I didn't draw or make things with clay. Instead of a book report, my English teacher once let me do a drawing based on *A Tale of Two Cities.* That was my first illustration job!

I especially liked drawing people involved in outdoor activities and, in fact, I was very active in sports myself. After high school, I went to Vanderbilt University on a football scholarship. In addition to sports, there were a lot of sororities and fraternities at school that provided me with an active social life as well. But after two years, I left home to study painting at the Art Institute of Chicago.

For four years, I was totally dedicated to painting and drawing. My hard work paid off when I graduated with a major fellowship. That award gave me enough money to allow me to move to New York and pursue my career as an artist. I didn't know anybody there but I knew that it was where all the major galleries and publishers were located. I felt the need to test myself against the very best competition.

My first jobs were for *Esquire* magazine. I did illustrations for CBS and Columbia records. My work also appeared in *Seventeen* and the *New Yorker.* Later, I even traveled a lot for *Sports Illustrated* magazine, painting and writing articles about fishing in Mexico and Central America. I've been in the marines and I've taught art at several schools, including the University of Kansas.

Now, retired from teaching, I've established a studio overlooking the Plaza in Kansas City. Here's where I'll continue illustrating and writing children's books. After traveling, living in different places, and interacting with many wonderful people, I'm able to draw on things I know for my books. And I like that.

"You don't 'become' an artist. If you 'are' one, get the most out of living as an artist. There's no model for that. You must always practice."
—*Thomas B. Allen*

The Baseball Player.
Age 7.
Pencil, 5 x 7".

Where do you get your ideas from?

Like everyone, when I read a story, I get images of what a place is like and how the people feel and move. My job is to get those pictures out of my mind and onto paper.

Ideas come directly from possibilities in the story itself. If I do a book, it is because the story has something I can feel strongly about illustrating. I draw upon my own experiences to help the reader share in the feelings, the time, place, and atmosphere that are appropriate for the story.

Some ideas come during the first, most important phase: research.

Sometimes they come from a memory that's been triggered by a passage in the story. Sometimes they just show up. If I've fed my mind enough information about a project, it will keep working on any problems I might be having no matter what else I am doing and—voilà!—an idea!

What is a normal day like for you?

When I was teaching, my "normal" days might have included classes, meetings, airport trips to pick up visitors who were coming to speak at the school, lots of phone calls, research, sketching, making storyboards or dummies for a book, doing finished pieces of art, checking proofs to see if the printer got everything right, reading manuscripts, writing letters, office visits with students, handling family matters, et cetera. I didn't have a "normal" day. Now that I've retired to devote myself to children's books, my days are less confusing, if not "normal."

Where do you work?

Everywhere. I prepare artwork in my studio but the process of creating it isn't limited to a particular space. Ideas may come to me in the kitchen or while I am walking in the woods. I do my research wherever I can find appropriate reference material. That might be in my den or the library, in a museum or out in the countryside.

Do you have any children? Any pets?

I have three children, Hilary, Missy, and Ivo; and two grandchildren, Jake and Vicky. My youngest daughter, Hilary, draws well and is an outstanding musician. I think she was born with the arts.

What do you enjoy drawing the most?

People. I've always thought of landscapes and cityscapes as stage settings for people. People provide the drama. I make up all of the people in my books, preferring to develop my characters from memory and observation rather than finding the characters and photographing them.

Do you ever put people you know in your pictures?

No, but sometimes I'll think of someone I know when developing a character.

Climbing Kansas Mountains by George Shannon. 1993. Pastel, 17 1/4 x 10 3/4".
Published by Bradbury Press.

What do you use to make your pictures?

Mostly I draw with charcoal and color with pastel and colored pencils on tinted paper. Again, research is important since I cannot make up a covered wagon or a locomotive or grain elevator. These may only be background props for the human drama, but they must be authentic.

How did you get to do your first book?

I showed my portfolio to an editor at a book publisher in New York. She liked my work and gave me a manuscript to read for my first "picture" book. It was called *When Windwagon Smith Came to Westport* by Ramona Weeks. Doing a book was different for me and fun. There were sixty-eight drawings done in a very direct, loose manner with pen and sepia ink. Some were dramatic, some poignant, and some humorous.

BIRTHDAY: January 28, 1963
Mary Jane Begin

MY STORY

I had a chalkboard from the time I was about five and loved drawing strange, birdlike characters and human faces for the "scribble game" my brother, Kit, and I invented. One of us made a scribble and the other had to make something of it. I'd draw my characters into scenes and stories.

When I was eleven, my family, along with my friend Susie's family, took a trip to Mount Washington. We climbed halfway up the mountain, swam in a river, crossed a rickety bridge on foot, and ate the best sundaes ever. Susie and I had crayons, colored pencils, and paper with us and we drew pictures of everything we did. They were some of the best drawings I'd ever created, probably because they were about things I'd actually done.

As a child I never thought I'd make art for a living. I didn't meet a working artist of any kind until I went to college. I intended to be a teacher so I "taught" my dolls, mostly English—never art—using that chalkboard. Now, I do teach art, at the Rhode Island School of Design (RISD, pronounced RIZ-D) and absolutely *love* it!

In high school, I made posters and banners for school activities and became known as "the artist" in my class. That made me feel special and unique. I made backdrops for plays, drew for the yearbook, and spent time going to art museums and learning to do watercolors and still-life drawings. I took as many art courses as I could and discovered egg tempera, gouache, watercolor, and acrylic paints. Fine-tipped brushes and pencils proved to be great for small details.

My mom was supportive about my plans for art school. So was my high school art teacher, Jill Berry, who told me that a career should not just be something you are good at, but something that is meaningful to you. I decided to go to RISD. When I told my mother, I was surprised to find out that her father, my grandfather Pepe Cote, had gone there in the 1930s.

I can't say I spent much time thinking about what life as an artist would be like. Adults said things like, "You'll wear a beret, live in a garret (I looked it up—it means attic), and you'll always be poor." But I was stubborn and believed that if I worked hard, I wouldn't be poor. Besides, berets and attics didn't sound so terrible. My high school chemistry teacher thought that I could have a promising career in science. In fact, I do use skills I learned in his class: research, problem solving, and experimentation. But, as much as I liked science, I loved to paint and draw. It made more sense to me to do what I loved rather than what I liked.

Probably more than any other work, Garth Williams's pencil drawings for *The Little House* books influenced me: The pictures and words together made me read avidly and care about nature, and people and places I had never seen. I had forgotten the strong emotions those books stirred up until I saw the work of Chris Van Allsburg at college and rediscovered my love for words and pictures.

Owls. Age 7. Tempera on construction paper, 18 x 12".

"Be stubborn. Some people will discourage you and think your choice
to be an artist is unwise. You'll know better."

—*Mary Jane Begin*

Where do you get your ideas from?

Reading the story many times, I try to see what the author intended. Words
hold different meanings for each reader, so my pictures "tell" a story differently
than those of another artist. Like a director with a script, I create characters,
costumes, sets, lighting, and scenes to produce a mood and express ideas as
every page turns.

Inspiration comes as I'm falling asleep. I'll jot down ideas in a notebook
before they slip away. Ideas from childhood, from silly things I see or hear, or
maybe from a single word. My best ideas are never forced; I give them a chance
to grow. Time is my best friend and my worst enemy: It lets me shape my best
ideas, but it's always passing . . . quickly!

What is a normal day like for you?

My day starts at ten or eleven (sometimes noon!), with coffee and the mail. If it's my turn, I walk our dog, Scout, and then get to work. My husband is an artist, too, and my best critic. He helps me work through painting or drawing problems. I usually work until five, eat supper, nap, then work until early morning, even daybreak if it's going well. I listen to music by day and television news or old movies at night. Some days, I also teach at RISD, speak at schools and libraries, and dig in my garden.

Where do you work?

My husband and I work together in a studio at home. I like the freedom of working barefooted or when I feel inspired or taking breaks if I feel like it. The worst thing about working at home is all that freedom! Phone calls, errands, or paying bills can interrupt the creative process and make easy excuses to procrastinate. Of course, I NEVER procrastinate.

Do you have any children? Any pets?

Our daughter's name is Gates Jacqueline. Scout is our high-maintenance beagle, named for a character in *To Kill a Mockingbird.* He needs lots of attention, affection, and W-A-L-K-S. (Unless I spell it, he'll think he's going out!) Oddly enough, I did *Before I Go to Sleep* years before we got Scout, but he looks just like the beagle in that book.

What do you enjoy drawing the most?

People and animals because of their movement. I try to catch one moment, to paint a snapshot of the story as it is in my mind. A friend calls my work "a photograph of my imagination." I want to convince readers that my characters are alive. Eyes interest me: the way light hits them and how flesh or fur curves around them. A brushstroke here or pencil mark there can completely change the character's expression.

Do you ever put people you know in your pictures?

Always. To define a character and how he or she behaves, I read and reread a story, write down descriptive adjectives, and think of someone whose walk, gestures, and looks fit the character. Aspects of the "person" may show up, even in an animal, place, or object. My mom was a bit concerned when I saw her as the perfect Porcupine for *Little Mouse's Painting,* perhaps because of Porcupine's rather full-figured shape!

What do you use to make your pictures?

I start in pencil on tracing paper, which I can see through to develop the drawing. Then I work on watercolor paper with brushes that can keep both a full shape and a perfect point. Doing a picture differently from anyone else is exciting. For *The Porcupine Mouse* and *Before I Go to Sleep* I used watercolor and colored pencils. To keep things interesting, I created the acrylic gloss and watercolor technique for *Little Mouse's Painting* and *A Mouse Told His Mother.*

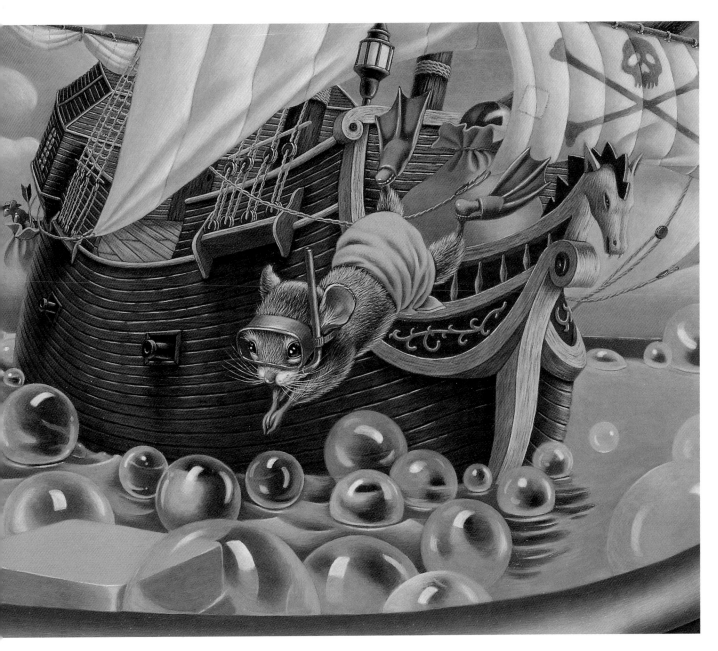

A Mouse Told His Mother by Bethany Roberts. 1995. Acrylic and watercolor, 16 1/2 x 9 1/4". Published by Little, Brown.

I was able to get deep, bright colors, but if the gloss isn't used continually, the paint cracks (it did!).

How did you get to do your first book?

In college I worked with an artist's representative (or rep) who sent slides of my art to publishers. Six months later, I got my first book, *Jeremy's First Haircut* by Linda Woolvard Girard, which was published by Albert Whitman and Co.

BIRTHDAY: January 8, 1959
Floyd Cooper

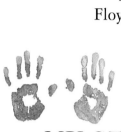

MY STORY • • • • • • • • • • • • • • • • •

I vividly recall my first drawing encounter as if it were only the other day. . . . I am three years old and my dad and I are out on a warm, sunny afternoon. Dad is busy building extra rooms onto our house. Sounds of hammer (not MC) echo across the countryside. Hey, what's this?!! I think Dad calls it "Sheetrock." It's like a chalkboard! Hey, it marks really well! Before I know it, I've drawn a very large duck on Dad's brand-new wall. Sheetrock is tough. My duck lasted through soap, through water, more soap, more water, and now, years later, I think it's finally disappeared!

I wasn't discouraged by Dad's reaction. I drew and drew and drew. Pastels and chalks became my favorite mediums. Eventually, I did graduate to using pencils and pens and paper. My mom had me practice writing cursive letters of the alphabet and doing other exercises with pens and pencils. Later, in school, my second-grade teacher once hung one of my paintings on the classroom wall. It was no big deal, though. She hung up every one of my classmates' paintings, too!

I realized that I had a special talent for art when I was nine, when I sold my first painting. Through a family friend, a nightclub owner bought it and hung it up, I was told, over the bar in his club. I was paid sixteen dollars! I began to paint and draw more than ever.

My teachers, especially art teachers, gave me much praise and encouragement. In seventh grade my art teacher dropped a stack of old anatomy books on my desk. I looked up, coughing through dust as my teacher muttered, "Read 'em!" and walked away. I took the books home and studied them thoroughly.

Drawing people has never been a problem for me because, I'm sure, of this teacher's actions. In fact, I began to win awards while I was in junior high and, finally, won a scholarship to the University of Oklahoma.

I started to get freelance jobs while I was still in college. I worked on a broad range of subjects. Once I had a job painting portraits at an auto dealership (buy a car, get a portrait). That job ended when a lady demanded, "Make me beautiful." I said, "I quit." I also painted a huge mural for a rally in Washington, D.C., illustrated textbooks, worked for an advertising agency, made small drawings for a dictionary, drew radio logos, and more. Then I got a job making greeting cards, which only left me time at night for my freelance work. Eventually I moved to New York and began to freelance full-time.

Great Grandparents' House. Age 9. Pastel and acrylic, 18 x 20".

"Be late one morning. When everybody gets upset and asks,
'What's wrong with you today? Hurry up!,' lean back, nose
in the air, and say, 'I am an arteeest!' Got it?"

—*Floyd Cooper*

Where do you get your ideas from?

People tell me that each book I do is different. That has a lot to do with the text. As I read a manuscript, I try to imagine, What is the weather? The time of day? What sounds can be heard? What are the smells? All to make it as real as possible. Atmosphere is everything! I like to travel, by plane, train, or book. And these elements feed the imagination, build it and strengthen it. A strong imagination goes a long way!

What is a normal day like for you?

A normal day for me is like a mirage. It can begin in a normal way: Raisin Bran sprinkled with Cap'n Crunch, Nintendo with my son, Dayton. Then poof! The phone rings and the image is gone. I like that each day ends up different from the one before. One thing is consistent—I juggle. You know, juggle: I work on several things at the same time. Over a recent period of several days I had to:

Write letters and return phone calls.
Answer phone; check messages on answering machine.
Work on paintings for next book.
Read manuscripts for new books.
Check schedule of books I will do.
Plan photo shoot. Meet kids who will model and their parents.
Work with a publicist on schedule for upcoming book tour.
Go to art store for supplies.
Visit school for program with kids.
Go to the library for research.
Catch a plane for out-of-state
    school and library visits.

Where do you work?

Before Dayton was born, his room was my studio. When he was old enough to want it, I had to give it up. Now I work in the "den." The TV is in there. Dayton is circling. . . . I think he wants the den!

Do you have any children? Any pets?

I have a son, Dayton. I used to think, how neat! We don't need pets! He rolls over great, but he doesn't fetch slippers. So I guess we'll get a dog someday. Maybe an Airedale. Yeah! Cool!

What do you enjoy drawing the most?

The anatomy books I read helped me understand muscles and bones, et cetera. So I'm very comfortable drawing people and capturing expressions.

Do you ever put people you know in your pictures?

Recently, I've been working from photos of kids who have posed for scenes I'm going to paint. Sometimes I use friends and family as models.

What do you use to make your pictures?

I use oil paints and kneaded erasers on illustration board. Sometimes I use professional models and a professional photographer, which helps me work faster.

How did you get to do your first book?

When I first came to New York, I couldn't find work anywhere. Then I got an agent who helped me find plenty of work. I was busy, working very fast. One job was different from all the others. It was to do a children's book called *Grandpa's Face* by Eloise Greenfield.

The Girl Who Loved Caterpillars by Jean Merrill. 1992.
Oil wash on board, 20 x 15". Published by Philomel.

BIRTHDAY: January 2, 1956
Julie Downing

MY STORY

I always loved to draw and paint but never set out to be an artist. My brothers collected Hardy Boys books, and written on the back of each was, "These books are perfect for boys from 8 to 14." I got angry that girls weren't supposed to read them, so I did and decided, at eight, to be a detective, too. I invented fantastic cases, set up a chemistry lab in my basement, and tested evidence. One summer, in a particularly difficult case, I pretended my neighbors' pool was poisoned and I had to neutralize the water to save them. So, I filled a bucket with every liquid I could find: ketchup, dishwashing detergent, salad dressing, and lots of food coloring. Climbing over our fence, I poured the stuff into the pool just as my neighbor came out for a swim. I got in a lot of trouble, and my career as a detective ended.

Next, I thought I wanted to be an ice-skater like Olympic star Peggy Fleming. Going to the rink every day to practice, I would begin by skating into the middle of the ice to wave to the audience (there was no audience!). I learned several waves, but not much else. I realized I wasn't a very good figure skater, but thought I would like to be in front of a real audience. So, at ten I decided to be an actress, and began doing a lot of community theater. I was a Lost Boy in *Peter Pan* and even Snoopy once, but my favorite role was playing Piglet in *Winnie the Pooh.*

Despite career changes, I never lost the magic feeling that comes from drawing and painting. I took lessons and even taught art to neighborhood kids. I wasn't the *best* artist in class, but I drew all the time and even won a few awards. Drawing even saved me in Biology. I got an A for my "excellent" drawings of what was under the microscope.

When I was a high school senior, I met someone who had gone to the Rhode Island School of Design. She told me it was a wonderful place where you could learn about lots of different kinds of art. It sounded so exciting. I finally realized I could be an artist. My guidance counselor paled a little when he heard my plan, then suggested a typing course in case I couldn't make it in art. I was mad. . . . I'd show him! I applied to RISD and swore I'd never learn to type.

Being around so many artists at RISD was both exciting and scary. I took painting, sculpture, and even a class in stained glass windows. Then I took a class about illustrating children's books and immediately felt at home. I'd found a way to combine everything I loved to do. Illustrating a book is like acting. I get to pretend to be different characters in a story. I am the director, deciding what happens on each page; I design costumes and scenery. I even use my detective skills to find what kind of clothes a shepherd might wear, or what a medieval king eats for lunch. I snoop through libraries, museums, antique stores, and even post offices to find a perfect chair, or the pattern of a castle floor. Of course, I get to draw, too!

Each book is a challenge. I love writing, researching, and illustrating. It is hard work, often frustrating, and at times a bit scary, but never dull. Sometimes I'm surprised that I became an artist, but I feel lucky to have a job I love. And when I decided to write my own books, I *did* learn to type.

Forest. Age 6. Crayon, 8 1/4 x 11".

"Don't be afraid to try new things, because each experience contributes to your art."　　　　　*—Julie Downing*

Where do you get your ideas from?

I write my own books, and illustrate books written by other people. Each book is very different and my ideas come from all different places. Some ideas come from my childhood, like *White Snow, Blue Feather,* the story of a simple journey on a snowy day. I began with sketches of snow and used my memories of winter.

　　I like to do books about things that interest me. I always listen to the music of Mozart when I work, and one Christmas I took a trip to Austria, where the composer had lived. The country was so beautiful, I wanted to draw everything. In Salzburg, where Mozart was born, I began a book about him. I tried to put myself in his place and imagine what he had thought and felt.

What is a normal day like for you?

Mornings are my favorite time, so I like to start work early. Every day is different. Some days, I spend the whole day at my drawing board. Other days I might do research at the library, take pictures of models, or run to the art supply store. I always work Monday through Friday, and sometimes on weekends.

Where do you work?

I live in a Victorian house in San Francisco that is about one hundred years old and painted green, turquoise, and two shades of pink. My studio in the front room has a wonderful bay window that lets in lots of light and gives me a great view of what is happening outside.

I have shelves and shelves of books in my studio, so I can research different things that I want to draw. Next to my desk is a supply cabinet. The top drawer holds over two hundred different colored pencils. I have a clipping file of pictures from magazines that I have saved. If I need to paint a sunset, I can just go to my file and look up *skies*.

Do you have any children? Any pets?

I have a daughter named Anna Louise. Unfortunately, I'm allergic to animals, so I never had pets. I love to draw animals and often use my friends' cats and dogs as models. But I have to be very quick when taking their pictures or else I start to sneeze like crazy!

What do you enjoy drawing the most?

I love to draw birds and animals. And people . . . especially if they are in costumes. I don't like to draw mechanical things like computers, rocket ships, or cars. If I ever have to draw a car, I try to put it way in the background so that it is really tiny. That way, you can't tell what it looks like.

Do you ever put people you know in your pictures?

I use my friends all the time, although I often make them older or thinner, or give them a different hair color. I like to invite people over for dinner, and ask them to pretend they are the characters in a specific book. I pose them, take photographs, and use the pictures when I am sketching my ideas. I also use people I don't know. I have hired real actors to pose because they are very good at pretending to be the characters. Sometimes I ask people to put on a costume. All the men who posed in *Mozart Tonight* wore sweatpants pulled up to their knees to look like knickers. My husband, Scott, and I pose a lot, too. I have modeled for a servant, a six-year-old girl, and even a troll.

What do you use to make your pictures?

I like to try different mediums. Although many of my books are done in watercolor, I have also done some with pastel and colored pencil. It really depends on the feeling I want to give to the illustration. If I am using watercolors, I work on very heavy watercolor paper. It is almost like cardboard. I do a light pencil drawing first and then paint with the watercolors. At the end, I might go back to the illustration and use a little colored pencil (it's very good for drawing hair) and some pastel to highlight the details.

How did you get to do your first book?

I had a lot of different jobs before I got to do my first book. After I graduated from college, I had a job dressing Snoopy dogs for displays; I designed posters for Macy's department store, and even had a job telling people how much their stocks were worth. On my vacations, I would go to New York City and show my portfolio to editors and art directors at book publishing houses. I got a lot of encouragement from people who liked my work. I was lucky to find an agent who liked my work, also.

While I lived in San Francisco, my agent showed my portfolio to all the

A Ride on the Red Mare's Back by Ursula K. Le Guin. 1992. Watercolor, 6 x 8". Published by Orchard Books.

publishers in New York City. She got me jobs illustrating textbooks and book jackets. Then one day she called and told me that an editor wanted me to illustrate a book called *Prince Boghole.* I was so excited. My husband and I had moved to England, and the story was about a princess who lived in an English castle. It was perfect. There was even a castle in the center of our town and whenever I needed to, I could walk down the hill and sketch it.

Denise Fleming

BIRTHDAY: January 31, 1950
Denise Fleming

MY STORY • • • • • • • • • • • • • • • • • •

I've always made things. For birthdays and special occasions I'd create personalized cards. At Thanksgiving I'd make clothespin Pilgrims and Indians gathered around a feast made of modeling clay. During my papier-mâché period, I made huge treasure eggs that opened, with brass hinges and clasps.

In school I decorated my papers and reports. After I discovered how much my teachers appreciated the extra effort (better grades) there was no stopping me. It was on to shaped reports. My report on George Washington was written on paper cut in the shape of George's head.

My dad had a basement workshop, where he made furniture. He created a space for me, helped me find art supplies, and even let me share his supplies. Once he bought me a pastel set the salesman said was really for adults. Dad told him, "My daughter is an artist." I felt very important.

My third-grade teacher liked my drawing of a sea captain so much that she recommended I take classes at the Toledo Museum of Art. I went every Saturday until ninth grade. Before class, my friends and I wandered through the galleries, making up fantastic stories to go with the paintings. When I was eleven or twelve, I had my first illustration printed. It was a painting of morning glories that was chosen to be the cover of a teachers' magazine. Still, I never really thought about being an artist. . . . Maybe it seemed too enjoyable to be a real job.

For a while, thanks to Laura Ingalls Wilder's books, I wanted to be a pioneer. My grandmother made me a bonnet. My bike was my horse. Next, I planned to be a veterinarian and collected injured animals. Then, I wanted to be a producer-director (I was bossy, so this had a lot of appeal). I directed neighborhood kids in plays, spook houses, circuses. My mom only let us charge buttons or pins as admission, which wasn't too promising financially. Once Charlie, a neighbor, tore all the buttons off his shirt so that he and his friends could attend one of my productions.

In high school, my art teacher suggested I enter an art competition for scholarship money. I began thinking of art as a career. I put together a portfolio, and won the scholarship money. In art school I began collecting children's books, but it was years before I realized I wanted to make them myself. Before then, I worked with my husband doing jobs like sign painting and designing lunch boxes.

For my first books I used my *rikki-tikki* style: short colored-pencil lines and watercolors. As I visited schools, I admired the large shapes and vibrant colors in children's paintings. My daughter, Indigo, made wonderful paintings full of color and movement. I tried different materials and techniques to get a similar effect. But every time I used a brush and paint I ended up painting *rikki-tikki.* One day I saw an ad for a papermaking class. It mentioned glitter. I love glitter, so I signed up. In class I found the technique I was looking for. I began experimenting, illustrating book ideas I'd had in my head for years. The samples I made in class became *Count!* Now I paint the pictures and write the words.

Where do you get your ideas from?

A phrase, words that rhyme, how an animal moves, or colors and patterns in my garden all may start me thinking. One idea leads to another and soon I have an idea for a book. Not every idea works and more than a few ideas end up in the wastebasket.

"Experiment—don't be afraid to try different materials and techniques."
—*Denise Fleming*

Kitties. Age 6. Crayon on paper, 11 x 8 1/2".

What is a normal day like for you?

My days vary. Some days I feel lazy. . . . I think, sketch, and work out ideas while still in bed. Other days I might mix paper pulp or cut stencils all day. Some days I work into the early hours of the morning on my pulp paintings or a book design. Some days I visit schools and bookstores. The only things I do every day I'm home are feed the animals, shower, eat, and drive my daughter to the stable. Oops, I almost forgot the do-nothing days that usually follow a couple of long, work-into-the-early-morning days.

Where do you work?

My husband, David, and I built a studio with lots of windows onto the back of our house. It's a pleasant place to work overlooking my gardens and bird feeders. I can take a break and watch the birds and squirrels, maybe even a rabbit or two. There are three large tables, two small tables, a desk, lots of cupboards, big buckets, vats of paper pulp, and a copy machine. The floor is linoleum over concrete, so water won't hurt it. Papermaking is very wet, messy work and paper pulp is everywhere.

Do you have any children? Any pets?

I have one daughter, Indigo. She was born in 1979. She writes wonderful poetry.

Do I have pets? Oh my, yes! . . . Warfy, a "schnoodle": part schnauzer, part poodle; Twitcher, a rabbit; Earl, a guinea pig; Fontaine and Dusty, the cats; E. B., a cockatiel; Misty, Maxine, and Buddy, our parakeets; and Indigo's horse, Erik, whose show name is Greatheart.

What do you enjoy drawing the most?

I like drawing bugs, birds . . . any kind of animal. I especially like close-ups. The painting of the ants and caterpillar in *In the Tall, Tall Grass* is one of my favorite illustrations.

Do you ever put people you know in your pictures?

Lots of times I am thinking of a certain person's personality and habits when I am sketching a hungry mouse or rambunctious rabbit.

What do you use to make your pictures?

My pictures are done with paper pulp. I make the sheet of paper and the picture at the same time. Sometimes I draw with squeeze bottles filled with pulp. It's like drawing a happy face on a sandwich with mustard from a squeeze bottle. I may add other material to the pulp for texture, like coffee grounds, boiled rhubarb, or horse's hair. Once I added oats and they sprouted. It made an interesting texture.

How did you get to do your first book?

I became friends with Wendy Watson, an author-illustrator of children's books. I told Wendy making books was something I wanted to do. She said, "Then do it." With her encouragement I put together samples of my art and flew to New York City to find book work. I was very lucky: one publisher liked my samples and gave me a story to illustrate.

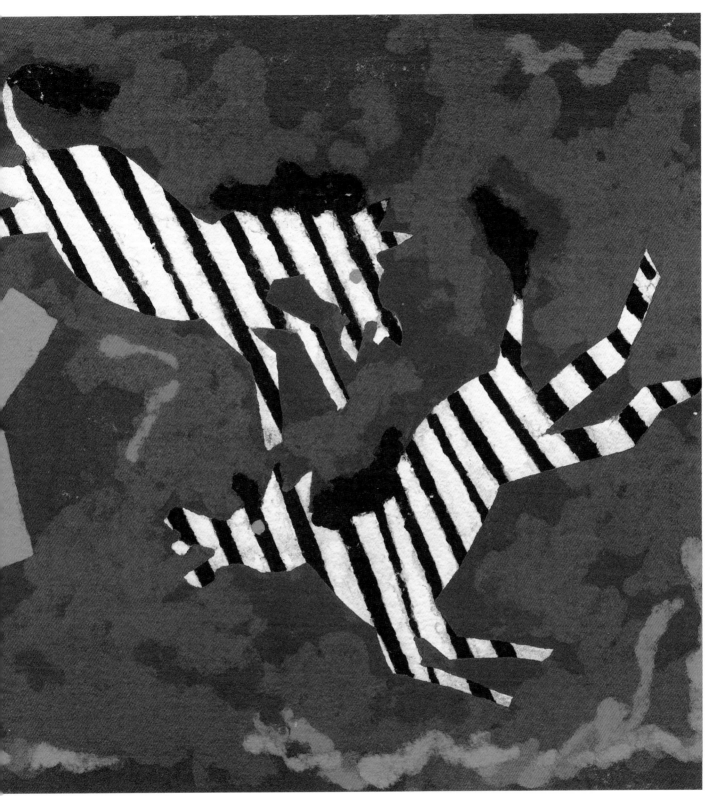

Count! 1992. Pulp painting, 25 x 15 1/2". Published by Henry Holt.

Sheila Hamanaka

BIRTHDAY: August 1, 1949
Sheila Hamanaka

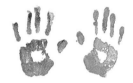

MY STORY •

I once did something I wasn't supposed to do: scribble in a book. It had beautiful drawings of horses, and I was crazy about them. I grew up on the Lower East Side of New York and the only horses I saw were police horses. My sister Lionelle and I took a few riding lessons, but my family was poor then and could only afford pony cart rides in Central Park. I thought I could learn to draw horses by copying over someone else's drawing. _What a shock!_ I couldn't even trace it! My lines went all over the place. . . . The pencil had a mind of its own! Drawing was harder than it looked but I decided to learn how to do it.

After I spent a few years drawing horses, people began telling me, "You're going to be an _artist_!" Words people say to you when you're a kid can have a big effect on you. My advice is to remember the good things, the kinds of things you like to hear about yourself. One of the main reasons I'm an artist today is that I liked the praise.

I was an expert at drawing blond women. My family is Japanese, but growing up, I rarely saw people of color in movies, magazines, or on TV. If I did, they usually played bad guys or servants. My father's an actor. Most of the small TV and movie roles he played were certain _types:_ the Japanese servant, the Chinese cook, the Alaskan Eskimo, the karate expert, et cetera. I never saw Asian actors playing a hero or heroine. All the cover models on magazines were European-Americans. So to me, beautiful women were always blue-eyed blonds. Of course, now I know that all people are beautiful!

Sometimes other kids made fun of me because I was Asian. They said mean things and pulled their eyes to slant upward. It really hurt my feelings until I learned to ignore such stupid behavior. Good artists must be able to draw people of all kinds, colors, shapes, sizes, and ages.

My ability to draw got me good grades on illustrated reports, posters, and dioramas. My second-grade teacher once let me take home red construction paper to trace and cut out cupids for a Valentine's Day display and I *accidently cut off one of their toes*! It seems silly now, but I was horrified then.

Later, at the High School of Music and Art, I took lots of art courses. In Art History, we only studied European art. So I discovered Japanese artists and all of the great Asian, Pacific, African, and Latin American art later. Whatever your cultural background, it may take digging on your own to uncover some interesting history and great art.

A mistake set me on the path to being an artist: My lousy scribbling provided a challenge; my love of horses kept me going. Pick something you love: cars, people, flowers, dinosaurs, et cetera, and keep drawing it. Artists have different strengths. Some use colors well, others put a lot of life and energy into their work. I thought that I would learn by looking: If I looked at the colors in the real world, in nature, my colors would look right, too. To draw realistic people or animals, it's important to study anatomy. (A race car driver must know what's under the hood and how it works.)

Kids know how to have fun. As a kid I absolutely loved to draw! Believe it or not, now that it's my job, I have to remind myself to enjoy it! Everyone tells kids, "Grow up!" They should also say, "Stay a kid at heart."

Pattern for Stuffed Horse. Age 10. Newspaper, 20 x 15 1/4".

"If no one tells you, 'You're going to be an artist,' then say it to yourself. Better yet, say, 'I am an artist.'"

—*Sheila Hamanaka*

Where do you get your ideas from?

From who I am, how I grew up, things I do. I was the youngest of five children. My mother was a secretary and my father an actor. I heard a lot of music and poetry at home. Artists of all kinds can influence one another so rhythms I hear in rock, rap, or jazz music may affect my pictures, which have rhythm, too. No two artists are alike. I feel it's important to look at art from all over the world.

I get inspired by a good book, a museum, or a concert. I get ideas while relaxing, going to the library, looking through old magazines, or by talking to different people. I find that real people and the lives they've led are more interesting than fiction. My uncle was a sumo wrestling champion and spent World War II in a prison camp. But unless you talk to him, you'd never know!

What is a normal day like for you?

My cats wake me up, we eat breakfast, and I start working. Sometimes I paint and sometimes I write or read or go check the library's picture collection for reference photos. After lunch, I work some more. I also try to exercise because I'm in a better mood with more energy if I do.

Where do you work?

My studio is in my living room. My apartment's small so I hang my drawings from a clothesline to see them all at once. As I work, I love looking out at trees on my street and the squirrels running along the telephone wires.

Do you have any children? Any pets?

I have two college-age kids: Suzuko lives in New York with me and my son Kiyo lives in Indiana.

I have two cats: Hudson, who wakes me when he wants breakfast, and Hemingway. Hudson does all the talking. I cook their food myself. Hudson's favorite is corn on the cob.

What do you enjoy drawing the most?

People and animals. The most important thing to me is character. For a humorous story my style is "cartoony," but I tend to paint realistically, as in *A Visit to Amy-Claire. Heart of the Wood* was more of a song, so I added funny characters in dancing scenes. For *Screen of Frogs* I drew real frogs at the

A Visit to Amy-Claire by Claudia Mills. 1992. Oil on canvas, 40 x 18".
Published by Macmillan.

Museum of Natural History, then added frog-personality to the drawings since
it was a folktale, not a science book.

Most importantly, I always try to draw different types of people—all
ages, colors, sizes, girls and boys—because we live in a multicultural world. I
don't want readers to feel the disappointment I felt as a child in not seeing
Asian-Americans in my picture books.

Do you ever put people you know in your pictures?
I use friends as models. They're easy to reach and I don't have to pay them.
People love to see themselves in a book but they expect the character to look

just like them. The fellow who posed as the woodcutter in *Heart of the Wood* is a well-known jazz drummer, and the violin maker is really a trumpet player but, ironically, the fiddler isn't really a musician. The cats are cats in real life: Hudson and Hemingway, of course!

What do you use to make your pictures?

I like to try different things. Mostly I paint in oils on canvas. They dry slowly and are easy to change. I also use colored pencil and acrylic paint. *Screen of Frogs* was done with collage so I could use all of the beautiful kinds of Japanese paper that I had found. Recently, I used pastel to achieve a soft look for another story. Someday, I would like to try three-dimensional art, comics, and animation, too.

I also use models. If I need to draw a girl on a bike, or a puppy, I will find models and take photos of them for reference.

How did you get to do your first book?

I met a children's book editor in an exercise class. She introduced me to the art director at her publishing house. I brought in samples of my paintings and drawings. Based on some of my pencil drawings of children, I was asked to do a book. I did one illustration for the cover but the art director thought my characters looked kind of cartoony. To get the characters to be more realistic-looking, I hired some models and did the whole picture over again. The book was called *Class Clown* by Johanna Hurwitz.

Kevin Henkes

BIRTHDAY: November 27, 1960
Kevin Henkes

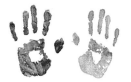

MY STORY

I've loved drawing for as long as I can remember. It's kind of like having brown hair and green eyes; being an artist is simply part of me. My oldest brother was an artist, too. I would try to copy his drawings and paintings. This was frustrating because he is five years older than me and could always achieve a level of expertise that I couldn't. He also used the nice thin brushes while I was left with the scraggly fat ones. (Being five years older has its advantages!)

I would often draw and paint at the kitchen table. In a family of seven this meant that I often worked with a lot of noise and activity going on all around me. But I didn't mind.

There was an art museum near my house. I took art lessons on Saturdays and during the summer. I loved the museum. It was the first place that I was able to see "real" art. Before that I had to rely on reproductions in library books. In the gallery I could see for myself how some people painted with thick, thick paint and others used thin washes. This was magical to me.

As I recall, the huge room in which the lessons were taught had a high shelf that held all sorts of objects. Things like animal skeletons, vases, dried plants, wooden pedestals, plaster busts, shells, and parts of machines. We would draw and paint the objects, sometimes. I can still remember how the room smelled. It smelled of paint and chalk and turpentine. It smelled dusty and spicy and sweaty on hot summer days. It was a wonderful smell.

When I drew at home I worked on small pieces of paper. At the museum, I worked on large paper for the first time. The museum also provided tall wooden easels. Standing before one of them, I felt like a professional artist.

At different stages of my life I liked to draw different things. I remember drawing cars, cartoon characters, and portraits of my next-door neighbor. My neighbor was also an artist, and one year younger than me. She was an expert at drawing horses; I was not. I remember drawing houses (complete with floor plans and measurements) that were hidden underground or inside mountains or floating in space. They had special features like doors that opened on command and dishes that washed themselves. I also tried to make up my own way of drawing people. I would draw the people in profile first and then try to draw them from the front.

I'm not certain exactly how old I was (perhaps eleven or twelve) when I wrote to Walt Disney Studios in California. I wanted to be an animator. I wanted to work for them. They didn't hire me, but they did send me a large envelope filled with pages of information on the history of animation and biographical information about Walt Disney. The label on the envelope had Mickey Mouse printed on it. You can imagine how excited I was when I saw it in the mailbox.

Sometimes I would place my drawings or paintings on the piano (where the sheet music goes), turn out the lights, and then shine a flashlight on them like a spotlight. I was pretending that I was a famous artist and that my drawings were in a show.

In high school I became very involved in track and cross-country. If there was a big meet approaching, I even forgot about art for a while. But not for long. Even now, on days that I draw a not-so-great picture or write a not-so-great story, I think that I'd like to do something else for a living. But I always come back to wanting to be an artist and writer. It's what I like to do more than anything else.

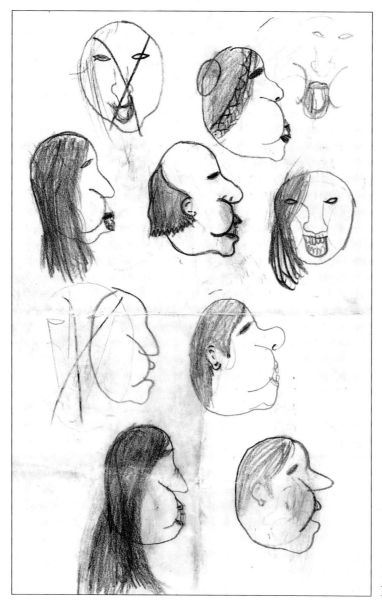

"Experiment a lot, have a good time, and don't worry about creating a masterpiece."
—*Kevin Henkes*

Faces. Age 9. Pencil, 5 x 8".

Where do you get your ideas from?

Many of my ideas come directly from my childhood. Although, of course, I use my imagination to give the ideas form and texture. I use my imagination to turn them into books.

I grew up in Wisconsin in a family of seven—one mother, one father, one daughter, and four sons. I'm the second youngest, so I knew what it was like to be the baby of the family for a while. But seven years after I was born I learned about being an older sibling—when my little brother joined the family.

Most of my books are about ordinary things: getting lost, adjusting to a new sibling, making new friends, starting school. Most of my books are about things I know.

What is a normal day like for you?

My daily schedule varies depending on what part of a book I'm working on. If I'm trying to come up with a new idea, my day might include: doing the laundry, vacuuming, washing dishes, or cleaning the blinds. If I'm writing or polishing a story, I'll try to be in my studio for at least two hours at a time, a few times a day. If I'm illustrating, I might be in my studio for eight hours a day, with just a few short breaks (and not much time for vacuuming, laundry et cetera).

If I've just finished a book, I like to do other things for a while. On those days you might find me painting large canvases, building funny sculptures, or trying to fix things in our old, drafty house.

But some things stay the same nearly every day. I usually get up early (by seven o'clock). My wife and I often run four miles with our dog before breakfast. We almost always walk the dog in the afternoon. And, I read for a while in bed each night.

Where do you work?

I work in a spare bedroom on the second floor of our house. It's a small, narrow room, but I like it because when I sit at my drawing table I can look out the window into our backyard. In the summer I can see our garden. In the winter I can watch our dog play in the snow. If I'm having a difficult time with a story or an illustration, I look up and count birds or the panes in the neighbors' windows. If I'm working at night and I look up, I see a reflection of myself. Because

the room is small, papers and books and folders are usually stacked on the floor in piles. I don't have a phone or a computer in my studio, but I have a radio. When I'm drawing or painting, I turn it on. When I'm writing, I don't.

Do you have any children? Any pets?

My wife and I don't have any children, but we have a dog and a cat. Our dog, Sadie, is part husky and part Labrador retriever. When I'm working in my studio, Sadie often lies in the hallway by the door. The hallway is carpeted and my studio is not. I think that's why she lies there.

Our cat, E. B., has long gray fur. She used to eat a lot and chatter a lot and follow us around from room to room. Since we got Sadie, E. B. eats more, chatters less, and follows us around about the same as before.

What do you enjoy drawing the most?

I suppose I like drawing mice the most. Not real mice, but mice that wear clothes and live in houses like the one I grew up in. The mice I draw go to school and tease their younger siblings. They ride bikes and play croquet.

The mice I draw are essentially people—that is, they do things people do, they talk the way people talk, and they feel things people feel. But I like to draw mice much more than I like to draw people.

Do you ever put people you know in your pictures?

When I've done books with people as characters, I've often asked people I know to model for me. The illustrations don't necessarily resemble the real people closely. I use models as a tool to help me draw. But sometimes I use the names of people I know in my books. The main character in *Sheila Rae, the Brave* is named after a girl who lived in my neighborhood when I was growing up. And Chester of *Chester's Way* is named after a relative.

What do you use to make your pictures?

Most of my illustrations are pen-and-ink drawings with watercolor washes. I do pencil sketches first. The paper I've been using lately is called Strathmore bristol board. One side of the paper is smoother than the other. I use the smooth side.

When I begin a new book, I usually buy new paintbrushes and pen nibs [little metal points that fit on to the end of a pen to allow you to draw in different widths]. But I still have some tubes of paint that I've used since I was in high school. And the container that I use for water is a red plastic Imperial margarine tub that I've used since I was in grade school.

How did you get to do your first book?

I was lucky. I had my first book accepted by a publisher when I was nineteen years old. During the summer after my first year of college, I traveled from my home in Wisconsin to New York City with three portfolios of my artwork and an idea for a story. The editor in chief of Greenwillow Books looked at my work and decided to publish my book *All Alone.*

Owen. 1993. Pen and ink, watercolor, 5 1/2 x 5 1/8". Published by Greenwillow Books.

BIRTHDAY: December 11, 1957
William Joyce

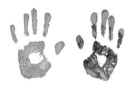

MY STORY • • • • • • • • • • • • • • •

My dad says I was born with a pencil in my hand. I always loved drawing. I started out drawing really ugly pictures of my sisters. That was my "Ugly Sister" phase. Then I had my "Dinosaur" phase. Then I had my "Dinosaur Eating Caveman" phase (I used a lot of red during that one, with guts everywhere). Then I had my "Dinosaurs Eating My Sisters" phase.

In school I could draw "Dinosaurs Eating Teachers" better than anyone else, so I got a lot of encouragement from classmates, but not from my teachers. Sometimes I'd draw stuff for school like "Ponce de León Looking for the Fountain of Youth in What Is Now Florida" and then I would get encouragement from my teachers. My parents even encouraged me. They let me take art lessons. There was never any talk about me growing up to be a rocket scientist or a plumber. It was apparent that I would be an artist no matter what. Of course, my parents thought I'd be poor, but that didn't bother them too much. As it turns out, I make more money than my dad, which is a big relief for me and a really big surprise for him.

I had two great art teachers: Mrs. Hogan and Mrs. Slagle. They were wise enough to just show me the possibilities and then let me figure stuff out by myself. If I got stuck, they'd help me out, but only when I was *really* stuck. They encouraged me to try all the mediums: watercolors, oils, pencils, pastels, charcoal, wood, canvas, paper. You name it. I liked some more than others. But knowing how to use them all is a big help. Some stories are better in pen and ink, some in watercolor or oil.

Then I went to college. I had already developed my art style, but in college some teachers wanted me to paint a different way. For some people that would have been okay. They might still have been looking for their style, but I knew what I wanted to do. So I got bad grades in art classes. Not for doing bad work, but because I wouldn't change. My parents thought it was stupid for people to try to make me change my style, too, so I quit art school and went to film school. I knew I wanted to tell stories and since movies tell their stories through pictures (they don't call them moving pictures for nothing), I thought I would learn a different way of doing my artwork. I studied animation a lot. Sometimes I would write a story and draw pictures to go with it. It seemed only natural after college to try to do children's picture books, so I did. The funny thing is now I'm working on movies based on my books. I love what I do. It's like getting paid for recess.

Dinosaur Mambo. Age 5. Oil, 6 x 12".

"Draw what you love and what makes you happy, not what others think you should. Stick to your guns (or your pencils) no matter what."
—*William Joyce*

Where do you get your ideas from?

My ideas come from everywhere. I never know what is going to spark a story. Sometimes it's an old monster movie, sometimes it's a song, a cartoon, something a kid says, a photograph, or something I see as I walk down the street. Usually it ends up being all these things sort of mixed together.

George Shrinks, for example, has stuff from the movies *King Kong, The Incredible Shrinking Man, Babes in Toyland,* and books like *The Borrowers. A Day with Wilbur Robinson* is sort of *The Day the Earth Stood Still* meets *Leave It to Beaver,* together with the book *The Great Gatsby* and things that happened to me when I was a kid.

What is a normal day like for you?

My baby daughter toddles in and wakes us up. I have breakfast and read the paper and think for a while in the bathtub. When I become so wrinkled that I look about a thousand years old, I get out of the tub and get dressed. Then I'll write or draw until lunchtime. Then I'll either go out to lunch or keep working.

   I listen to music while I work. If I'm working on a chase scene, I play really exciting music like "Ride of the Valkyries" or the *Batman* sound track. By 4:00 P.M. I'm completely out of my mind from being stuck inside so I go run amok all over town. Sometimes I get sane again and come back to work for another hour or so. Then I either force my wife to not cook dinner so we can go out to eat or we stay home and all run amok together. When we're all completely exhausted from running amok together, we fall asleep in front of the TV set and have very funny dreams.

Where do you work?

In my private fortress studio stronghold that has a secret password and is guarded by an attack cat named Doris Day, who lost her tail in an automobile accident.

Do you have any children? Any pets?

We have a little girl named Mary Katherine. We also call her "The Wonder Baby." We have a cat. We used to have some goldfish, but they ran away. We have a lot of lizards that live in our yard. A bunch of racoons live (uninvited) in our attic and play rugby at two o'clock in the morning several nights a week.

What do you enjoy drawing the most?

I like drawing robots, spaceships, monsters, and bugs the best.

Do you ever put people you know in your pictures?

I put people I know in almost all my books. The family in *Dinosaur Bob* is mine when I was little. My dad, sister, nephews, wife, and a guy named Cade Herzog posed for all the people in *A Day with Wilbur Robinson*. When my wife was pregnant, she posed for the egg in *Bently & egg*.

What do you use to make your pictures?

I use acrylic paints, pen and ink, oil paints, watercolors, colored pencils, and really fancy paintbrushes. I have some dinosaur models that I use when I'm drawing dinosaurs. I also have tons of books that I use. Books about trains and animals and whatever I might need to help me draw. For *Bently & egg* I got a frog and some goldfish at the pet store to use as models. The frog hopped away and I guess he took the fish with him, because I couldn't find them anywhere. But my cat looked like he gained weight while I was working on that book. . . . Hmmmm.

How did you get to do your first book?

It was in the second grade. We had a contest at my school to see who could write the best kids' book. Mine was called *Billy's Booger*. I did not win. I was sent to the principal's office.

When I was almost grown-up and out of college I went to New York, where most of the publishers are, and showed them my stuff. I even showed them *Billy's Booger* and they still gave me a job. My First Published Book was called *Tammy and the Gigantic Fish* written by James and Catherine Gray. It's a little bitty black-and-white book and it's actually okay.

Santa Calls. 1993. Acrylic, 16 x 16". Published by HarperCollins.

Maira Kalman

BIRTHDAY: November 15, 1949
Maira Kalman

MY STORY ● ● ● ● ● ● ● ● ● ● ● ● ● ● ● ●

One beautiful clear crisp and sunny day when I was eight or nine or maybe seven and a half no I couldn't have been that young I must have been ten I was sitting in a tree in Henry Hudson Park in Riverdale, New York, reading a book. And I knew.

I really just knew that I had this feeling that I was home. Not in the tree. In the book.

In the writing. In the paper.

It was all hyperreal and perfectly satisfying. I was going to be a writer. That was that.

Then I had a teacher named Mrs. Walters. She taught us composition and she said, "Maira, you have talent." That was definitely that. There was no doubt in my mind except that there are many doubts but that is something that goes with work.

So I started to think that I would be a writer.

My father was a businessman, and my mother was a housewife but that is a very small way of looking at it because my mother made me believe that art was definitely real and that you could be silly or strange or use your imagination and that was important.

My older sister who was tall and skinny decided that she would be an artist and when I was a little older I decided I could do that, too. And no one said I couldn't, so I did.

I went to college and studied literature. And I did not study art. I did not study medicine or law or physics. Then I put some drawings in a portfolio and started knocking on doors hoping that a magazine would hire me to illustrate a story. And many did not.

Then some did and some more and for a long time I forgot about writing and I spent many quiet hours in museums looking at paintings that I liked and did not like. Then I decided that I would be an artist who told stories with pictures. Narrative drawing. That was that. Then I had a story inside me and wrote my first children's book.

By then I had had two children inside me and then outside me and they made me think about writing books and they call me Moom.

I look for surprises and wait for the mistakes and hope they all add up to a book. I love making books, holding books, walking down the street with a book under my arm.

Divine object.

Where do you get your ideas from?

Looking and listening. Dreaming. Daydreaming. Reading. Watching movies. Daydreaming some more. Talking to myself. Eavesdropping. Dreaming.

What is a normal day like for you?

First thing read the obituaries to remind myself that I am still alive. With coffee. Go to my studio. Sit down to write. Leave studio. Wander around city. Take pictures of funny, nice, strange stuff, people, places. Go to a museum. Drink more coffee. Come home. Play with the children. Put the children to bed. Put myself to bed.

Chicken under Tree in Israel. Re-creation of 1956 drawing. Colored pencil, 8 x 10".

"Trust your instincts. Keep working. Search for the truth. Have fun. Travel. (Love it.)"

—*Maira Kalman*

Where do you work?

My corner studio at home. Cafés. Museum gardens. Libraries. Airplanes. Backyards. Coffee shops. Skating rinks. Swimming pools. I don't like to stop writing. Not always on paper. Often in my head. But I am unable to turn the process off.

Do you have any children? Any pets?

My children, Lulu and Alex, are growing every day. And they wanted a dog. But I am allergic to dogs. So we bought a bird named Barney. And we taught him to bark. So everyone is happy.

What do you enjoy drawing the most?

I love to draw umbrellas, lemons, and ladders. Then I see a person with a green beard and I have to draw that. I love to draw what pops into my field of vision and makes me happy. That is always unknown and a surprise and that is why I do it.

Do you ever put people you know in your pictures?

I have put 439 people in my drawings. There are 62 on a waiting list and I may draw them if they wear the right clothes or have good hats on. I met Bruno at a waterfall. He was doing invisible paintings of people swimming and I asked to see the paintings and he said, "Here they are" and I said "Where?" and he said "Here" and I looked surprised and his wife, Marlene, said, "Don't you know what Bruno does? He paints invisible paintings." People who I include in my books say, "Well, it's about time" and people who I don't include say, "When are you going to do something smart and include me in your books?" My husband's mother is patiently waiting for me to include her little dog Dorca instead of that stupid Max dog.

What do you use to make your pictures?

Paper, brush, gouache. Then I tear or rip out pictures from magazines. And see things in books. And then I take pictures with a little Leica camera that fits in my pocket and then I make sketches around the city or anywhere and ideas pop in and I sketch and then draw. I make a dummy of the book before I make the final paintings.

How did you get to do your first book?

David Byrne, of the music group Talking Heads, and I collaborated on a book called *Stay Up Late,* a song from his album *Little Creatures.* It was my husband, Tibor's, idea. He is a book designer. And he said, "There are parents and kids who like this song and you like this song." And fortunately Tibor and David and I had worked together doing art for Talking Heads. David thought it would be funny and nice. And it was!

It is often hard for me to look at my own work. I can see the things I don't like and I get embarrassed but I also say to myself that I will make it better next time. What is better? Different. Exploring language. Simpler.

Max in Hollywood, Baby. 1992. Gouache on paper, 14 x 17".
Published by Viking Penguin.

Deborah Nourse Lattimore

BIRTHDAY: May 16, 1949
Deborah Nourse Lattimore

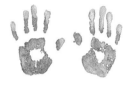

MY STORY

There wasn't a single person in my family who didn't draw or paint. But I did it the most. There was a work of art or a statue on or against just about every wall in our old Spanish house in Beverly Hills: huge marble statues in each corner of the living room, a bronze horse and rider by the fireplace, and family portraits everywhere, many of them life-sized. I constantly got a good look at art.

I was raised by my grandmother, who painted with me every day after lunch. We drew in the garden; we drew in museums. Everything about ancient peoples interested me and I've always felt more at home with them than with modern people. The Taj Mahal could have been Sleeping Beauty's castle; Tutankhamen was a handsome young prince. My bedtime stories might have been about a stone butterfly in Poland, a house with chicken feet in Russia, or a Mayan falling into a well of death.

If I ran out of paper, I drew on the wall in our dancing patio behind a large Mexican tapestry. I drew chariot races, mummies, friends and family all dressed up. I started doodling on that wall when I was about four. No one could see my artwork. The tapestry hid it, so I thought I was safe.

When I was about twelve, my grandfather took me aside and said that it was time to work strictly on paper. So I did. I never had enough paper and I never will, probably. I draw all the time. The urge to look constantly at things and draw is like being bitten by an annoying bug. Once bitten, there's no escape; being an artist is something you have to do. If not, you feel off-kilter and crummy.

In elementary school I was chosen to attend a special Saturday art class. I immediately got a crush on my handsome young art teacher. He gave me extra paper to take home and taught me new techniques. He got me into art shows and still guides me in my work. He especially taught me to be happy about mistakes, those "happy accidents" that lead to ways of working I might otherwise never try.

At fourteen and again at seventeen, I attended Art College of Design, in Los Angeles, California, on scholarship. I didn't like the style of painting I saw people doing then so, after briefly trying premedical studies, I changed to art history and archaeology. I didn't know where this might lead but I tried every kind of art I could: cartography, or mapmaking; archaeological and medical illustration; television, fashion, and newspaper art. You name it, I may have tried it.

No one told me how to get a job as an artist. I just went to places where artists seemed to work and asked for a job. I worked for companies as an artist for several years, and spent evenings doing what I really wanted to do: illustrating books. After many attempts on my own, I took a class with Diane Goode, a children's book illustrator, and began to understand how books were made.

"Being an artist is something you feel as well as do. Your art should be best just for you, before anyone else sees it. Trust your feelings and remember: Erasing and starting over is an art form, too . . . a good one."
—*Deborah Nourse Lattimore*

Minotaur. Age 11. Linoleum block print in two colors, 4 x 6".

Where do you get your ideas from?

Mostly from associations I make with people, objects, places, or smells (perfume, smoke in a fireplace, newly made soap); I look at, listen to, or breathe something and let my thoughts drift away. An idea's always lingering. Museums get me going. I love paintings, murals, statues, small art objects. . . .

What is a normal day like for you?

There is no such thing. With two children, I tend to work around my time with them. I drive them to school in the morning and home in the afternoon. I manage to write and illustrate, usually between 9:00 A.M. and 2:00 P.M. and then again from 9:30 P.M. to 3:00 or 4:00 A.M., depending on how tired I am.

Where do you work?

My studio is a small converted garage behind my house, with industrial-looking, eight-foot-long lightbulbs. Drawings and notes are pinned up all over. Prints from my books decorate the walls along with art done by my children, silly cartoons sent by friends, a photo of a brilliant cellist named Jaqueline du Pre (I play cello for fun), and an old photo of the actor Laurence Olivier. Hubba, hubba! I have a new drafting table, and things roll off of it frequently. So I am often picking up pencils and other things.

Do you have any children? Any pets?

My children, Nicholas and Isabel, interrupt me all the time. They can be very cute so I don't need any other pets but, in fact, we have parakeets: two English budgies, George and Gracie, and two American ones, Zoe and Zack.

What do you enjoy drawing the most?

Whatever I'm working on at the time. I love variety, so I approach each book as if I'd never drawn before or used certain color combinations. I also have a definite interest in the ancient world. What I crave most about it is the sense of

Why There Is No Arguing in Heaven. 1989. Watercolor, 16 x 10".
Published by HarperCollins.

mystery the modern world seems to lack. Seeing something in a book or museum that is hundreds or thousands of years old, I love it immediately. It has lure; it has secrets. Can I, a person of this century, discover those secrets? I want to explore them, draw them, write stories about them. I try to weave tantalizing pieces of the past back together, always aware that some pieces can never be found. That excites me.

Do you ever put people you know in your pictures?

Sometimes I draw my children, to surprise them later on. They usually think Old Mom's pretty weird. My books are mostly about ancient peoples. When my kids see I've drawn them as ancient Irish people avoiding Vikings or as New Zealanders sticking out their tongues, or chasing each other in old, fancy French costumes, they think I've got a slightly odd sense of humor.

What do you use to make your pictures?

Pencils, gouache, watercolor, and inks. I've printed backgrounds with cut potatoes, sea sponges, and even finger paint.

I research to find the earliest information on a subject that I can. In *The Flame of Peace,* I re-created Aztec codices, fifteenth- and sixteenth-century books made by and for the Aztecs. For *The Winged Cat,* I translated hieroglyphs (I've studied Egyptology), reproduced the style used in the *Book of the Dead,* and even painted pages to look like ancient papyrus. In *The Sailor Who Captured the Sea,* I drew the Irish monastery of Kells by using the original plans, which I found at the UCLA Research Library.

How did you get to do your first book?

I showed *The Flame of Peace* to a classmate at UCLA who sent me to an editor she thought might like my work. I'd been rejected so many times that when the editor said she liked it, I assumed it was just a very polite rejection. But she accepted me! I was so surprised I called her up later to be sure she meant it and she said, "Yes!" Pretty good feeling.

BIRTHDAY: August 28, 1961
Brian Pinkney

MY STORY

I grew up in an artistic family. My father was an illustrator and my mother was a jewelry maker, hat designer, and writer. My two brothers and sister and I played musical instruments, and we were always drawing, painting, or building things. One of my favorite hobbies was making little men out of pipe cleaners and colored wire. I built airplanes, spaceships, and cities out of cardboard, wood, and anything else I could find. Then, I would make up action and adventure stories that lasted for weeks. After a while, I'd take everything apart and build something new.

I always knew I wanted to be an illustrator because I wanted to be just like my father. I did everything he did. My desk was a miniature version of his desk. My paintbrushes and pencils were the ones from his studio that were too old or too small for him to use. I had a paint set like his and a studio like his. But my studio was in a walk-in closet, which made it the perfect size for me.

I didn't have formal art lessons from my father. When I came home from school, I stopped by his studio to tell him about my day. He kept on working as we talked. One day he was painting a picture of a night sky with a large brush and watercolors. He began by laying down a light brown wash across the whole picture. When it was just about dry, he painted another wash over it with bright blue watercolor. After repeating this process a couple of times, he had created the richest deep blue sky I had ever seen. After a visit like this, I would go to my little studio in the closet to try out the techniques I had learned.

My schoolteachers were very supportive of my interest in art. Even though they didn't like the little robots and tiny men I drew running up and down my notebook pages, they did encourage me to draw and paint for extra-credit projects. I made posters for the science room showing how a tadpole becomes a frog. I drew a poster showing all the bones of the human body. For Social Studies I wrote a report on Leonardo da Vinci. He became an idol of mine because he was an artist, musician, and inventor, and he was left-handed, like me. For extra credit I drew some of da Vinci's inventions and his portrait. Because he was left-handed, he wrote all of his notes backward. I started writing all of my notes backward, too. But when it came time to study for a test, I couldn't read them so I held my notebook up to a mirror.

In college I got the opportunity to experiment with different mediums and techniques. I worked in pen and ink, watercolor, oil paint, and acrylics. Printmaking was one of my favorite classes because I was able to work on etchings and lithographs. Years later, at the School of Visual Arts in New York, I grew restless with watercolor. An instructor suggested I try scratchboard. I used it to make a little portrait of myself riding a bike. . . . *Wow!* It was like drawing, etching, and sculpting all at the same time. From that moment on, I started using scratchboard for all my illustrations.

I try to grow with each new book. My early pieces were dark because of the black in the scratchboard. But I add colors now so my work is brighter.

African Dancer. Age 9. Watercolor, 8 1/2 x 7".

"Make pictures of things you like."
—*Brian Pinkney*

Where do you get your ideas from?

My ideas come from books I've read, experiences I've had, things I've seen. I spend a lot of time daydreaming about ideas I want to make pictures about. When they are clearly in mind, I sketch them in the sketchbook I always keep with me. If I'm doing a picture and get stuck for an idea, I do other things to free my mind. I practice Tae Kwon Do [a Korean martial art], play my drums, wash dishes, or take a nap. When I least expect it . . . *Boom!* An idea hits me and I run to my studio.

What is a normal day like for you?

I wake up around 9:00 in the morning, think about all of the things I want to do, roll over, and go back to sleep. I get up around 9:30, brush my teeth, shower, and get into my studio by 10:30. I look at everything I want to work on, then go for a long walk and a subway ride. I take a Tae Kwon Do class, wander around New York City, eat lunch, and get home around 4:00. I make some phone calls, play my drums, look over my work, then go lie down on the couch to clear my head. I wake up at 5:00, work until Andrea comes home from her job around 7:30, kiss her hello, then work until dinner at 8:30. After dinner and light conversation with Andrea, I work until 1:30 in the morning, brush my teeth, and go to bed.

Where do you work?

Mostly, I work in my studio in my apartment in Brooklyn, New York. When I'm sketching, I often like a change of scenery, so I grab my sketchbook, hop on the subway, and go to the park, the museum, or the beach.

Do you have any children? Any pets?

My wife, Andrea, and I don't have any children . . . yet.

What do you enjoy drawing the most?

I love drawing people and I enjoy making pictures about the African-American experience.

Do you ever put people you know in your pictures?

Always. I've used my parents, brothers, sister, nieces, nephew, and friends in pictures. My favorite models are Andrea and myself. For *Alvin Ailey,* a picture book written by Andrea, we realized we had to become dancers to get a feel for Alvin Ailey and his dancers. We took dance classes for months. Once our dance techniques were perfected, Andrea modeled for Katherine Dunham and some of the other dancers and I posed for Alvin Ailey.

What do you use to make your pictures?

I work in scratchboard, oil pastels, and oil paint. Scratchboard is a technique that uses a white board covered with black ink. A drawing is "scratched" into the ink with a sharp tool to reveal the white underneath. I add color with oil pastels and oil paint, wiping away excess pastel or paint. It's like what I did in grade school when I'd cover a piece of paper with black crayon, then scratch out a drawing with a Popsicle stick.

Sukey and the Mermaid by Robert D. San Souci. 1992. Scratchboard and oil pastels, 19 x 10 3/4". Published by Four Winds Press.

How did you get to do your first book?

At the end of my senior year, a writer came to my college looking for a student artist to illustrate his story that was set in Africa. The author looked at a few portfolios and decided to use me. The book was called *The Story Teller* by Derrick Gantt.

Vera B Williams

BIRTHDAY: January 28, 1927
Vera B. Williams

MY STORY • • • • • • • • • • • • • • • •

My parents believed all children had art talent. There was no money for lessons for me and my sister so we drew a lot at home. But when I was seven my amazing mother moved us across the street from this "heaven" called Bronx House. There in the afternoons and long days of summer I painted, acted, danced, played baseball, and wrote for our newspaper. I met artists who taught for the WPA, a government program.

When I was eight my painting *Yentas* (Yiddish for gossips) was shown in the Museum of Modern Art. I went to see my work alongside art from WPA classes all over the U.S.A. I was standing beside my painting hoping everyone knew it was mine when Mrs. Roosevelt herself appeared. While she and I discussed the meaning of the word *yenta,* cameras filmed us for the weekly newsreel to be shown in neighborhood cinemas.

I got quite stuck-up over that. And then the *New York Times* asked me to do a Christmas painting. My Jewish family didn't celebrate Christmas but like any illustrator I used my imagination. With my five dollars pay, I bought a new coat and hat. (Most people then didn't earn five dollars in a day!)

After that I was invited to attend special Saturday art classes. My sister and I took the subway downtown to spend a few hours with wonderful big sheets of paper, fine brushes, paint and chalks galore. I remember several Pied Pipers I painted there. Something about the haunting old story got my imagination working just as certain stories still do.

We were encouraged to express whatever was in our imagination. Our teacher frowned on copying, but I always loved to copy and even traced illustrations from my books.

At Music and Art High School, I got to study art history and still-life painting, and to create my first long picture book. But the best part was the other young people who talked about, thought about, and made art. By my senior year I felt I might like to be a children's book writer and illustrator.

At Black Mount College in North Carolina, I did study graphic art. I learned to use the printing press. I made a book there that I hand bound. I even wove the cloth for the cover! Our college was unique. We all worked together to grow our own food and build our own buildings, as well as study subjects. I was interested in so many activities that it was a long time till I actually took up illustrating and writing as a real career. I think that was partly because young women were not encouraged to have careers other than marriage, as they are now.

A lot of my first art projects were done for causes I believed in (such as preventing nuclear destruction). I did posters, magazine covers, and illustrations as my contribution. But my first actual career was being a parent. This included storytelling and arts and crafts. I helped start a school and taught art, making books for and with the kids. I did my first book for publication only when I was forty-seven and my children were grown-up, but these many experiences have been important for my work.

I have different kinds of imagination. One filled with colors and design, the other busy with people and their stories. I can create the world I believe in on the pages of a book. I'm the boss! In my books people of all colors can live together; girls as well as boys can go on wilderness adventures; everyone can have experiences worthy of a book. A child I see, who perhaps has no chance to do art, can wind up in my book as a young artist like Bidemmi in *Cherries and Cherry Pits.* It's hard to match the excitement of creating these 32-, 40-, or 48-page worlds!

> "Make a lot of pictures,
> play with the colors,
> look at a lot of pictures,
> daydream, imagine."
> —*Vera B. Williams*

The Pied Piper.
Age 9 or 10.
Paste paint, 5 x 7".

Where do you get your ideas from?

Like all artists, I'm very hospitable to ideas. Imagination, memory, dreams, everything we experience constantly produces ideas. Ideas knock on everyone's door but many people send them away. When I'm in a certain mood, ideas just come. I made *"More More More," Said the Baby* when I was just in love with my new grandchild. I could hardly *not* write. If I'm empty of ideas, I go for a walk and the sights pick me up and inspire me. The subway is like a museum of people. Sometimes I doodle in my notebook and surprise myself with where my sketches may lead. . . .

What is a normal day like for you?

It's hard to get days to be "normal." I love going for walks, seeing my friends, sitting down with a newspaper. Sometimes I need to go to public meetings. Once I'm out, I want to do this and that, arranging my day however I want. When I'm beginning a book, I will sometimes work very long days. I find that I can only do my best, most imaginative work for a few hours at a time. But I'll work longer on finishing a piece and might rework a picture many times, even too much. Sometimes I look at my work and say, "Why didn't I stop?" Then, when I look at it the next day, I'll realize that I got what I wanted.

Where do you work?

I did my earlier books right where I ate breakfast and served dinner. I was always having to move things around, which made working crowded, but possible. I did several books in summer places that I rented. The first book, which I did in watercolor, was done on a houseboat I had in Vancouver, Canada. The boat rocked, but not so much that I couldn't paint. It had a little built-in drafting table and that was what made me decide to take it. People could look right into your boat and you got to know everyone. When the book was finished, I had a party on the dock and hung my drawings up on clotheslines.

Music, Music for Everyone. 1984. Watercolor, 11 1/2 x 9 1/2".
Published by Greenwillow Books.

Now, I have a studio that I really like, in a place I can get messy. I have a mirror so I can model for myself. There's a lot of wall space, which I need since I make many versions of the same piece and like having my work all around me.

Do you have any children? Any pets?

I have three grown children and five grandchildren. I don't have pets now. I've had cats and dogs. When my children were little, we had a horse, pigeons, rabbits, mice, various birds, and guinea pigs.

What do you enjoy drawing the most?

Probably people. If I'm doodling, I'll draw very active people like children and grown-ups dancing or skipping. I'll sketch while I'm at a meeting, doodle all over my notes. Sometimes I go to a drawing group where we have live models.

Do you ever put people you know in your pictures?

I put a very special dog I knew named Potato in a story once. And someone *like* my grandson Hudson is in *"More More More," Said the Baby.* I am more likely to borrow people's names but I make up my characters. I actually think that some of my characters look like me.

What do you use to make your pictures?

I use watercolor a lot. For *Three Days on the River in a Red Canoe* I used colored pencil to make it look like a travel notebook. In *Cherries and Cherry Pits* I used Magic Marker on some pages and watercolor on others, because a girl in the story makes many of the drawings and I knew she would use Magic Markers.

For *"More More More," Said the Baby* I used tempera paint that was almost as thick as ice cream. For a recent book I made small, loose, sketchy pictures in ink with a brush. I've studied some Japanese calligraphy and have done a lot of black-and-white drawings. Black ink on white paper is exciting. It can look so clear and definite!

How did you get to do your first book?

A friend of mine, a wonderful illustrator named Remy Charlip, showed me ideas, sketches, and a dummy for a book he didn't have time to do. I wanted to give it a try and he generously gave me the chance. I had done magazine covers, paintings, leaflets, and posters but I'd only done books for my own kids. In the course of raising and teaching children you do a lot of art. I'd made quilts, masks, costumes, dolls, and even baked a bread motorcycle! In fact, I became so imaginative at making gingerbread houses that I wrote a book about them.

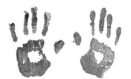

David Wisniewski

BIRTHDAY: March 21, 1953
David Wisniewski

MY STORY • • • • • • • • • • • • • • • •

When I was little, my mother showed me how to connect circles and ovals to form human bodies. Like this:

I drew these "bubble men" a lot, especially with spearguns and air tanks in dramatic underwater battles with huge sharks. I didn't see the need for faces or fingers (or even clothes!). I was thrilled just to have shown *action.*

That changed when I started reading comic books. At first, I liked DC Comics' cast of characters: Superman, Batman, Wonder Woman, The Flash. But then I discovered Marvel Comics. They sported more intriguing heroes and villains like Spiderman, Doctor Doom, The Fantastic Four, and Sub-Mariner plus a more exciting art style: shadowy, textured, and cinematic.

I drew these characters freehand, trying to get the proportions and muscles correct. But my comic-book art education didn't help me draw women very well. Mine always had Batman's big jaw and broad shoulders.

Though I enjoyed drawing, I didn't think of becoming an artist. I thought being a scientist would be more fun. My friend John changed my mind. He drew amazingly funny cartoons about protozoa doing crazy things.

They made me laugh so hard at lunch that milk came out of my nose. I tried doing them, too. Together, we cracked up most of the seventh grade with our single-celled humor.

I found that art could help me make friends and be accepted, a major discovery for a chubby, nearsighted kid who got picked last for sports. I did cartoons and pen-and-ink drawings in high school, too, but my real interest was in theater and performing in plays and musicals.

After graduation, that interest led me to Ringling Bros. and Barnum & Bailey Circus Clown College. In eight weeks, I learned juggling, unicycling, mime, makeup, and acrobatics. I performed with Ringling for two seasons, then joined Circus Vargas for another year. Performing every day taught me a lot about hard work and showmanship, but I grew tired of life "on the road" so I headed home.

I took a puppetry job with the parks department and Donna Harris, the lovely woman who hired and trained me, became my wife. We decided to start Clarion Shadow Theatre, a touring puppet company. We specialize in shadow puppetry, a form of theater over two thousand years old. We've modernized it by using overhead projectors and cinematic storytelling techniques.

I didn't realize it then, but preparing shadow plays gave me skills I would need later to make books. Turning the myths and folktales of different cultures into scripts made me a better writer. Making shadow puppets and scenery made me comfortable telling a story with pictures. And my cutting skills certainly sharpened!

When we stopped touring to raise our children, I began doing freelance illustration. First, I used simple black silhouettes. Then, I added color and depth to achieve the cut-paper style I do today. So, you see, no one thing led me into illustration. After learning skills from circus and puppetry, I found I had to alter them to succeed in picture books.

Shark Attack. Re-creation from the artist's "bubble men" period. Pencil, 8 1/2 x 11".

Where do you get your ideas from?

I ask, What's the point of the story? What's the moral? Then I locate a culture and time period that supports the point of the story and research it. Since *The Warrior and the Wise Man* showed that thinking through a problem was better than fighting, I set it in medieval Japan to contrast fierce samurai knights with peaceful Buddhist monks.

Through research, I absorb enough information for my imagination to roam responsibly within a culture. Research allows bits of history, folklore, and custom to find their way into the story. Details about architecture, clothing, tools, and games fill the pictures.

Usually, the local library has enough resources. But *Sundiata: Lion King of Mali* required the National Museum of African Art's specialty library and expert staff for more accurate illustrations. The cultural attachés of foreign embassies can also be a big help.

What is a normal day like for you?

It varies. If I'm working on a book, which is most of the time, I can spend the whole day in my studio. If I'm doing freelance work, I go to magazines or ad agencies to discuss the job with art directors. If there's a puppet show, Donna and I load the van with equipment and zoom off. Then, some days I visit schools as a guest author and illustrator.

Where do you work?

I did have a loft studio in Laurel, Maryland. It was great having a place I could get messy. When paper shreds piled up, I took out "Jaws," an industrial-strength vacuum cleaner. ("Jaws" was pretty powerful. It accidentally sucked up paper I needed, and might have gotten a telephone repairman, too.) Now I have a home studio.

Do you have any children? Any pets?

Yes. Ariana draws a cartoon strip called "The Hairy Heels" about a skinny family who bounce on springy hairs growing from the soles of their feet. Alexander invents things out of string; like a door-closing device that almost gave me a black eye.

We have three cats: Amber, a calico; Asher, who is gray and one-eyed from fighting; and Sunny Jim, an orange Siamese mutant.

What do you enjoy drawing the most?

People, especially in dramatic "good versus evil" situations with lots of tension and atmosphere. I have the hardest time with horses, because I can't always get their legs to look right.

Do you ever put people you know in your pictures?

No. My books all take place in different cultures and time periods. Using friends and relatives, even in minor roles, just wouldn't work. Who would believe my Uncle Bob as an ancient Maya nobleman?

What do you use to make your pictures?

Usually, I cut Color-aid papers. They come in many colors and I don't have to paint them first. I also use textured surfaces like charcoal paper or bark paper for different effects. Instead of wet glue, I use double-stick photo mounts [the adhesive pieces of paper that hold photographs in albums] to hold my illustrations together. If I need depth between layers of paper, I use double-stick foam tape. To get even more depth, I place slices of mat board or Fome-cor behind layers of paper. To cut, I use an X-Acto knife and a *lot* of #11 blades. I use between eight hundred and a thousand to do the sixteen illustrations in one book! To protect my table, I use a special plastic mat under my paper that seals up if you cut across it.

Sundiata: Lion King of Mali.
1992. Cut-paper, 18 x 12".
Published by Clarion Books.

How did you get to do your first book?

I met an agent who advised me to show my work to publishers in New York. She advised me to have a story in mind, either an original or a retelling. I set up appointments in advance, then tried to come up with a story. I finished typing *The Warrior and the Wise Man* the morning of my interviews. The first editor really liked my art and asked if I had a story. I read it to her. When I finished, she nodded and said, "You just sold yourself a book."

SECRET TECHNIQUES ••••••••••••••••••

Thomas B. Allen:

I do lots of research, lots of sketches, and a pencil dummy to show how the story flows. I'll change viewpoints and scale, which gives a sense of movement: one page a bird's-eye view from afar, then a close-up. I don't want my readers bored.

Mary Jane Begin:

I had trouble making water shimmer until I found that putting a highlight next to a dark area in a puddle, droplet, or wave helped to make the water look wet. Putting a highlight next to a light area of the water makes it disappear or look like dull metal. The contrast of the lightest light next to the darkest dark is what gives the illusion of reflection.

Floyd Cooper:

You'll need:

       1 burnt umber oil paint (from a tube)

       5 tablespoons turpentine substitute (Permtime or Turpenoid)

       1 #10 round sable paintbrush

       1 sheet of illustration board (15 x 20")

       Spray fixative (or hair spray as a substitute)

       1 4" sponge brush

       1 medium kneaded eraser

Mix and stir paint and turpentine substitute together in a bowl. Blend with #10 brush until creamy (like tomato soup without the crackers). Spray your board with fixative. Using 4" sponge brush, spread oil mixture across the board evenly (tilting board if necessary to get a smooth, even coating). Let it dry to the touch, about 15 minutes. Using the kneaded eraser, lift out highlights or even draw right into the paint. Work until done. But sshhh! It's a secret!
Makes 6–8 servings (or 2 paintings)

Julie Downing:

In kindergarten, I liked to draw clothes on a clothesline. One day a friend showed me how drawing one leg slightly to the side made a pair of pants look like it was blowing in the wind. My drawing looked like it was moving! It seemed like magic. Here's how:

No wind.
Legs are straight.

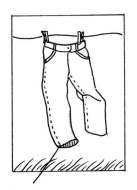

Breeze.
Legs slightly bent,
drawn a little to side.

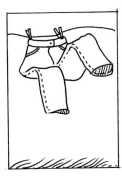

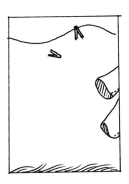

Big wind.
Legs folded—drawn
much further to side.

Tornado.

Denise Fleming:

I use finely shredded cotton rags to make a fiber I can float in water. Then I pour this mixture onto a screen. The water drains through the screen; the paper pulp (fiber) stays on top of the screen. To make pictures, I cut stencils (like this rabbit stencil) and pour pulp into the cutout areas.

Pour pulp

Sheila Hamanaka:

When you draw someone from the front, the eyes will look like this:

I always drew women from the side, so I drew their eyes from the side, too, like this:

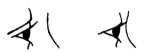

To draw Asian eyes, draw them like this:

My older sister, Wendy, showed me that eyes should go in the very middle of a head, halfway down the face, like so:

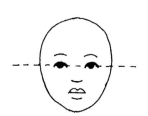

Hint: A lot of professional illustrators keep a picture file. Cut out interesting magazine pictures and make different files for the pictures: Animals, People, Places, Cars, and so on.

Kevin Henkes

Over the course of time, I've realized how powerful a few simple lines can be.

Look how easily you can create different expressions on the mouse:

Happy

Sad

Angry

William Joyce:

I do have a secret technique. I like my colors to look like the colors in really old movies. Old movies were actually four different colors of film stuck together.

Red, yellow, blue, and black. So I paint my pictures in kind of the same way. First I do yellow. Then thin layers of red on top of that. Then blue and then

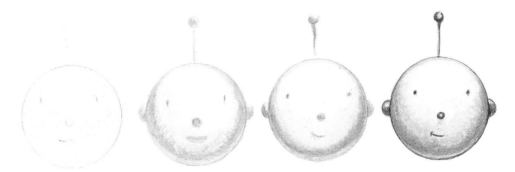

black or dark brown.

Maira Kalman:

Look at something.
Close your eyes.
Draw that thing with your eyes closed.
Open your eyes.
Draw that thing but don't look at the paper only at the thing.
Close your eyes.
Draw anything you feel.
Keep doodling as much of the time as you can.
Carry a sketchbook with you and a pen.

Deborah Nourse Lattimore:

Is trying to draw something making you crazy? Scribble it. Loosen up. I've solved lots of problems by "fooling around." If you're doing a face at an angle

you aren't comfortable with, try this:

Scribbling a face   could become a raised face . . . profile . . .   or getting really loose   getting tighter
(Experimenting)   (fewer lines)   (more lines)

Brian Pinkney:

1. First I "scratch" a simple line drawing onto black scratchboard.
2. Then I "scratch" away the background.
3. Finally I "scratch" in the details.

Vera B. Williams:

I try to work on a picture that is close to how I feel on a particular day. If I feel a bit sad, I'll work on a page in the story that needs to show that feeling. Once I did a scene of a dance right after I came home from a party and the music was still in my ears. That's a good way to do your art because the colors and expressions of the characters can come right from your own moods. It takes a long time to do a book and it shouldn't become a chore. You want every page to "come alive."

David Wisniewski:

Here is an easy way to layer paper like I do:

Get Scotch Double-Sided Foam Tape from an office or school supply store. Cut a shape out of construction paper (a bird, a flower, a building . . . anything). Cut strips of foam tape, stick them to the back of your cutout, then stick the cutout to whatever background you want. This automatically raises the cutout so that it casts a shadow.

Experiment with using more than one layer of foam tape to raise the cutout higher. Or, place one cutout in front of another (like a bird flying past a building).

BOOKS BY THE ARTISTS ••••••••••••••••

All the artists were asked to name four or five favorite books that they've illustrated. If the artist didn't also write the book, the author's name is given, so you'll be able to find it in your library or bookstore.

Thomas B. Allen

Climbing Kansas Mountains by George Shannon. Bradbury Press, 1993.
The Days Before Now by Margaret Wise Brown. Simon & Schuster, 1994.
In Coal Country by Judith Hendershot. Alfred A. Knopf, 1987.
On Granddaddy's Farm. Alfred A. Knopf, 1989.
Sewing Quilts by Ann Turner. Macmillan, 1994.

Mary Jane Begin

Before I Go to Sleep by Thomas Hood. Putnam, 1990.
Little Mouse's Painting by Diane Wolkstein. Morrow Junior Books, 1992.
A Mouse Told His Mother by Bethany Roberts. Little, Brown, 1995.
The Porcupine Mouse by Bonnie Pryor. Morrow Junior Books, 1988.

Floyd Cooper

Brown Honey in Broomwheat Tea by Joyce Carol Thomas. HarperCollins, 1993.
Coming Home. Philomel, 1994.
Jaguarundi by Virginia Hamilton. Scholastic, 1995.
Meet Danitra Brown by Nikki Grimes. Lothrop, Lee & Shepard Books, 1994.
Pass It On compiled by Wade Hudson. Just Us Books, 1993.

Julie Downing

Daniel's Gift by M. C. Helldorfer. Bradbury Press, 1987.
Mozart Tonight. Bradbury Press, 1991.
The Night Before Christmas by Clement Clarke Moore. Bradbury Press, 1994.
A Ride on the Red Mare's Back by Ursula K. Le Guin. Orchard Books, 1992.
White Snow, Blue Feather. Bradbury Press, 1990.

Denise Fleming

Barnyard Banter. Henry Holt, 1994.
Count! Henry Holt, 1992.
In the Small, Small Pond. Henry Holt, 1993.
In the Tall, Tall Grass. Henry Holt, 1991.
Lunch. Henry Holt, 1992.

Sheila Hamanaka

All the Colors of the Earth. Morrow Junior Books, 1994.
The Journey: Japanese Americans, Racism, and Renewal. Orchard Books, 1990.
Screen of Frogs. Orchard Books, 1993.
Sophie's Role by Amy Heath. Four Winds Press, 1992.
The Terrible Eek by Patricia Compton. Simon & Schuster, 1991.

Kevin Henkes

All Alone. Greenwillow Books, 1981.
Chrysanthemum. Greenwillow Books, 1991.
Clean Enough. Greenwillow Books, 1982.
Julius, the Baby of the World. Greenwillow Books, 1990.
Owen. Greenwillow Books, 1993.

William Joyce

Bently & egg. HarperCollins, 1992.
A Day with Wilbur Robinson. HarperCollins, 1990.
Dinosaur Bob and His Adventures with the Family Lazardo. HarperCollins, 1988.
George Shrinks. HarperCollins, 1985.
Santa Calls. HarperCollins, 1993.

Maira Kalman

Hey Willy, See the Pyramids. Viking Penguin, 1988.
Max in Hollywood, Baby. Viking Penguin, 1992.
Max Makes a Million. Viking Penguin, 1990.
Ooh-La-La (Max in Love). Viking Penguin, 1991.

Deborah Nourse Lattimore

The Dragon's Robe. HarperCollins, 1990.
The Flame of Peace. HarperCollins, 1987.
Frida Maria: A Tale of the Old Southwest. Brown Deer, 1994.
Punga, the Goddess of Ugly. Harcourt Brace, 1993.
Why There Is No Arguing in Heaven. HarperCollins, 1989.

Brian Pinkney

Alvin Ailey by Andrea Davis Pinkney. Hyperion, 1993.
Dear Benjamin Banneker by Andrea Davis Pinkney. Harcourt Brace, 1994.
Max Found Two Sticks. Simon & Schuster, 1994.
Seven Candles for Kwanzaa by Andrea Davis Pinkney. Dial, 1993.
Sukey and the Mermaid by Robert D. San Souci. Four Winds Press, 1992.

Vera B. Williams

A Chair for My Mother. Greenwillow Books, 1982.
Cherries and Cherry Pits. Greenwillow Books, 1986.
"More More More," Said the Baby. Greenwillow Books, 1990.
Scooter. Greenwillow Books, 1993.
Stringbean's Trip to the Shining Sea. Greenwillow Books, 1988.

David Wisniewski

Elfwyn's Saga. Lothrop, Lee & Shepard Books, 1990.
Rain Player. Clarion Books, 1991.
Sundiata: Lion King of Mali. Clarion Books, 1992.
The Warrior and the Wise Man. Lothrop, Lee & Shepard Books, 1989.
The Wave of the Sea-Wolf. Clarion Books, 1994.

•••••••••••••••• **ACKNOWLEDGMENTS** •••••••••••••••••

Grateful acknowledgment is given to the artists who participated in this book, for permission to reproduce their photographs and samples of their childhood artwork. Our appreciation, too, to the following individuals and publishers.

Page 5. Drawing by Kalila Minor.

Page 15. From *Climbing Kansas Mountains* by George Shannon. Illustrations copyright © 1993 by Thomas B. Allen. Reprinted by permission of Macmillan Books for Young Readers, an imprint of Simon & Schuster Children's Publishing Division.

Page 21. From *A Mouse Told His Mother* by Bethany Roberts. Illustrations copyright © 1995 by Mary Jane Begin. *A Mouse Told His Mother* is forthcoming from Little, Brown and Company in Fall 1995. By permission of Little, Brown and Company.

Page 27. From *The Girl Who Loved Caterpillars* by Jean Merrill. Illustrations copyright © 1992 by Floyd Cooper. Reprinted by permission of Philomel Books.

Page 33. From *A Ride on the Red Mare's Back* by Ursula K. Le Guin. Illustrations copyright © 1992 by Julie Downing. Reprinted by permission of Orchard Books.

Page 35. Photo credit: David Powers

Page 39. From *Count!*, written and illustrated by Denise Fleming. Copyright © 1992 by Denise Fleming. Reprinted by permission of Henry Holt and Company, Inc.

Page 44. From *A Visit to Amy-Claire* by Claudia Mills. Illustrations copyright © 1992 by Sheila Hamanaka. Reprinted by permission of Macmillan Books for Young Readers, an imprint of Simon & Schuster Children's Publishing Division.

Page 47. Photo credit: Laura Dronzek

Page 49. Photo credit: Ned Vespa

Page 51. From *Owen*, written and illustrated by Kevin Henkes. Copyright © 1993 by Kevin Henkes. By permission of Greenwillow Books, a division of William Morrow & Company, Inc.

Page 57. From *Santa Calls*, written and illustrated by William Joyce. Copyright © 1993 by William Joyce. Reprinted by permission of HarperCollins Publishers.

Page 59. Photo credit: Andreas Sterzing

Page 63. From *Max in Hollywood, Baby* by Maira Kalman. Copyright © 1992 by Maira Kalman. Used by permission of Viking Penguin, a division of Penguin Books USA Inc.

Page 65. Photo credit: Copyright © 1991 by Marilyn Sanders

Page 67. Photo credit: Barry L. Schwartz

Page 68. From *Why There Is No Arguing in Heaven* by Deborah Nourse Lattimore. Copyright © 1989 by Deborah Nourse Lattimore. Reprinted by permission of HarperCollins Publishers.

Page 71. Photo credit: Andrea Davis Pinkney

Page 75. From *Sukey and the Mermaid* by Robert D. San Souci. Illustrations copyright © 1992 by Brian Pinkney. Reprinted by permission of Simon & Schuster Books for Young Readers, an imprint of Simon & Schuster Children's Publishing Division.

Page 80. From *Music, Music for Everyone* by Vera B. Williams. Copyright © 1984 by Vera B. Williams. By permission of Greenwillow Books, a division of William Morrow & Company, Inc.

Page 87. From *Sundiata: Lion King of Mali* by David Wisniewski. Copyright © 1992 by David Wisniewski. Reprinted by permission of Clarion Books/Houghton Mifflin Company.